BALANCE

THE CENTER IS NOT ALWAYS THE POINT OF BALANCE. WHEN YOU
FIND THAT PLACE WHERE BALANCE IS ACHIEVED, PEACE WILL RESULT
IN ALL SITUATIONS. THERE IS NO CONFLICT, FOR EVERYTHING RESTS
WITHOUT STRAIN.

CALMNESS

IN ALL ACTIVITY, PRACTICE CALMNESS. TO REMAIN CALM AMIDST
THE CHAOS OF LIFE REQUIRES A TREMENDOUS AMOUNT OF FOCUSED
ENERGY. BE CALMLY ACTIVE AND ACTIVELY CALM.

CLARITY

BE CLEAR IN ALL THINGS. AS A CALM POND REFLECTS THE FULL
MOON PERFECTLY, LET YOUR ACTIONS REFLECT YOUR SPEECH AND
YOUR SPEECH REFLECT YOUR ACTIONS.

COMPASSION

FEEL THE PAIN OF OTHERS. UNDERSTAND THEIR STRUGGLES AND
DISAPPOINTMENTS, THEIR HARDSHIPS AND INADEQUACIES, AND OPEN
YOUR HEART TO THEM. REALIZE THAT EVERYONE IS DOING THE BEST
THEY POSSIBLY CAN. JUDGE NO ONE. BUT RATHER, CRADLE ALL OF
HUMANITY IN YOUR HEART.

成

Concentration

As a drowning man wants air, as the lover seeks their beloved, this is the way you must focus on that which you want. This intensity of concentration will remove all obstacles.

CONTENTMENT

REJOICE IN WHATEVER LIFE GIVES YOU. CRAVE NOTHING ELSE.
KNOW THAT WHATEVER YOU HAVE BEEN GIVEN IS FOR YOUR OWN
HIGHEST GOOD.

_____

_____

_____

_____

_____

_____

_____

_____

_____

_____

_____

_____

COURAGE

FIND THE COURAGE TO HOLD ON TO YOUR BELIEFS, EVEN IF THE
WORLD AROUND YOU CHOOSES TO BELIEVE DIFFERENTLY. HAVE THE
COURAGE TO CHANGE THOSE BELIEFS THAT NO LONGER FIT THE PERSON
YOU HAVE BECOME. IN DOING SO, YOU TRULY BECOME YOURSELF.

成

DANCE

IN DANCE, NO MOVEMENT OR DIRECTION IS BETTER OR WORSE THAN
ANOTHER. THIS, TOO, IS A WAY TO VIEW ALL OF LIFE. SEE ALL
THE "GOOD AND BAD" THINGS THAT HAPPEN TO YOU SIMPLY AS
MOVEMENTS IN THE DANCE OF LIFE.

DESTINY

You can look . . . and you will find it. You can not look . . . and you will find it. That which is yours will surely come to you.

Ego

Those who say they know, do not know. Those who say they do not know, also do not know. Therefore, be quiet and let your actions speak for you. They speak much louder than your words anyway.

FRIENDSHIP

To love people who love you is easy. Choose to be everyone's friend, whether they like you or not. When you love and accept others as they are, you will have friends everywhere.

和

_____

_____

_____

_____

_____

_____

_____

_____

_____

_____

_____

GRACE

THE BEAUTY OF GRACE IS THAT YOU RECEIVE BLESSINGS FOR NO
REASON. AS ABOVE, SO BELOW. PRACTICE RANDOM ACTS OF GRACE.
GIVE TO OTHERS FOR NO REASON, OFFER KINDNESS TO THOSE WHO
ARE UNDESERVING, LOVE THOSE WHO NO ONE ELSE LOVES.
PRACTICE GRACE.

成

HAPPINESS

HAPPINESS COMES FROM WITHIN. IF YOU CHOOSE TO BE HAPPY, NO
ONE AND NO THING CAN EVER TAKE THAT HAPPINESS FROM YOU.

HUMILITY

THE WAY OF THE EARTH IS TO EMPTY THAT WHICH IS FULL, AND FILL
THAT WHICH IS EMPTY. TRUE HUMILITY BRINGS GREAT FORTUNE.

Inner Peace

Inner peace brings fulfillment. Attain it, and life works.
Give it away, and happiness becomes elusive.

The Journey

Understand that the journey is as important as the destination.
Enjoy every moment, and live life fully. This is Zen.

成

JOY

JOY IS INSIDE YOU. NOT IN ATTAINMENT OF THINGS DESIRED, NOR IN THE ACHIEVEMENT OF GOALS MADE, BUT IN THE SIMPLE FEELING THAT LIES WITHIN YOU. KNOW THAT THIS JOY IS UNAFFECTED BY OUTER CIRCUMSTANCE, AND JOY WILL BE YOURS FOREVER.

Kindness

Through kindness, the world softens. Be kind to all beings and things. In this way, creation returns to its natural state of beauty.

LOVE

ALL BEINGS WANT TO BE LOVED AND ACCEPTED. THAT IS SOMETHING YOU CAN GIVE TO THEM. LOVE COMPLETELY, UNSELFISHLY, AND UNCONDITIONALLY.

LOYALTY

BECOME LOYAL TO YOUR INNERMOST TRUTH. FOLLOW THE WAY WHEN
ALL OTHERS ABANDON IT. WALK THE PATH OF YOUR OWN HEART.

和

Nonjudgment

To straighten what is crooked, you must first straighten yourself. Once you are aligned, the whole world looks different.

PATIENCE

WATCH WATER DROP ONTO THE ROCK BENEATH IT. ONE DROP DOES
NOTHING, BUT MANY DROPS OVER TIME CREATE A HOLE IN THE ROCK.
SUCH IS THE POWER OF PATIENCE.

成

PEACE

To create peace in the world, you must be unruffled within.
Become tranquil, walk in stillness, and act in harmony.
The serenity that radiates from you will create peace.

THE PRESENT

THE PAST IS OVER. THE FUTURE WILL NEVER COME. NOW IS THE
ONLY MOMENT THAT WILL EVER EXIST. THEREFORE, LIVE EACH
SECOND TO THE FULLEST.

Problem Solving

THE WAY TO REMOVE DARKNESS FROM A ROOM IS SIMPLY TO TURN
ON A LIGHT. IN THE SAME WAY, TO RID YOURSELF OF ANY DIFFICULTY,
CONCENTRATE ON THE SOLUTION RATHER THAN THE PROBLEM.

PROSPERITY

PROSPERITY IS NOT IN WHAT YOU HAVE ATTAINED BUT RATHER IN
WHAT YOU GIVE AWAY . . . FOR IT IS ONLY WHEN YOU BECOME EMPTY
THAT YOU CAN BE FILLED WITH SOMETHING GREATER.

和
和
和
和
和
和
和

REFLECTION

WHEN THE POND IS STILL, THE REFLECTION IS CLEAR. WHEN THE
MIND IS STILL, THE REFLECTION OF LIFE IS CLEAR. REFLECTION
BRINGS CLARITY.

Renunciation

Each day, accept everything that comes to you as a gift. At night, mentally give it all back. In this way, you become free. No one can ever take anything from you, for nothing is yours.

Right Action

Strive to always do what is right—not in the eyes of others, but in your own heart. Others' thoughts are transitory— one moment they will love you, the next they will not. Act on what is right in your own heart, and there will be victory.

Right Speech

Say little. But when you speak, utter gentle words that touch the heart. Be truthful. Express kindness. Abstain from vanity. This is the Way.

和

Right Thought

You are what you think. Think it today, become it tomorrow. Nothing can help you or hurt you as much as the thoughts you carry in your head.

Self-Acceptance

Your true nature is neither good nor bad. It is not found in enlightenment or lost in delusion. It is the spotless beauty of all creation. Who then is the self you are accepting or not accepting?

Stillness

When the night is still, you can hear the silence. When the mind is still, listen to the silence and let it guide you.

成

Success

Success is not found in what you have achieved, but rather in who you have become.

和

TRANQUILITY

TRANQUILITY IS ACHIEVED WHEN YOU ARE IN HARMONY WITH
ALL BEINGS AND ALL SITUATIONS, KNOWING THAT EVERYTHING IS
PRECISELY THE WAY IT IS MEANT TO BE.

TRUTH

WHAT IS, IS. WHAT IS NOT, IS NOT. NO AMOUNT OF WISHING OR
WANTING CAN CHANGE THAT SIMPLE FACT.

和
和
和
和
和
和
和

_____

_____

_____

_____

_____

_____

_____

_____

_____

_____

_____

Understanding

What happens to you does not matter; what you become through those experiences is all that is significant. This is the true meaning of life.

成

UNITY

UNITE ALL THINGS. WHEN ALL OF YOUR ENERGIES ARE GOING IN THE SAME DIRECTION, GREAT THINGS WILL HAPPEN. WHEN YOU UNIFY OTHERS, SUCCESS IS ASSURED. WORK IN HARMONY WITH THE WAY, AND ALL THINGS WILL FLOURISH.

WISDOM

TREAT EVERYONE AND EVERYTHING WITH LOVING COMPASSION. WHEN
YOU SEE NO DIFFERENCE BETWEEN THE SACRED AND THE PROFANE,
THE SAINT OR THE SINNER, THAT IS THE ULTIMATE WISDOM.